Just Peace Society
With Chef D Malfi

Prayers and Poetry with a Purpose

Daniella Marie Malfitano

India | USA | UK

Made with ❤ on the BookLeaf Publishing Platform
www.bookleafpub.in
www.bookleafpub.com

Dedication

For the people who have lived, lost, and loved through it all.

This book was written for You in mind to find.

I pray this book and this inspirational work gives you hope and feeds your spirit, body, and your mind.

Preface

In this creative work of healing and nourishment, I will delve into my discovery of how my pursuit for peace has been developed through my art in all forms including literary, culinary, visual, spoken, musical, poetic, and prophetic. Within these pages, I use my aesthetic quest for wisdom in the form of prayers and poems of purpose to illustrate through my divine calling, artistic expression, and culinary and literary vocation. These are some of my life learnings and how the truth has manifested through my faith and my food, as a powerful tool for inner and outer world transformation. Perhaps the perfect formula for building just peace on planet earth and beyond as is our mandate from God.

Within, I offer a written meal, if you will - a selection of spiritual sustenance. Each page as a reflection of my wisdom quest. In using these artistic selections to enumerate and expand upon the human pursuit of truth telling through art. It is through these expressions that can my conviction best begin to illustrate what the journey has taught me through the life-affirming initiation as life is.

To help me clarify my evolving approach to wisdom, I have chosen what writing to showcase in order to establish what wisdom means to me throughout my life's story. Each of these offerings have impacted, contributed, and transformed my life through living in an earnest and continuous truth pursuit. It is my hope that each entry speaks to you clearly! These works informed my creative world, and link together universal truth telling and living obediently and authentically.

This work fits into the larger frame of the world in that it is a highlight of how creative expressions are all pointing to that which resonates within the spiritual, aesthetic, and moral imagination we each carry and have a contributing part in. It is at this nexus of art and activism through truth of the familiar ride of life that one can understand that passion and purpose come from within. This experience and this journey is a holy quest for wisdom of living in abundance.

I chose prose to share in an authentic way without restriction, ad libitum. I find it important and my responsibility to use art to share truth which supports the collective pursuit for peace. This is the expression and beauty of being human, and of belonging to the larger story of life, to find wisdom within and to learn to reveal and share your light. In other words - to know and trust our pain to reveal our greatest purpose.

Acknowledgements

Collēcta - Introductory Bites

***In the name of the Father Mother, Son and Sis, and
loving Holy Spirit;***

It is great to have you in my life in every way these days.
I can say with full confidence that I've never felt this
level of security, peace, and conviction in my spirit
in the way that I do now –
and I attribute all of that to
my prayerful relationship with you.
To start every day,
every meal,
every connection,
every conversation,
with you leading the way –
I want everyone to know that I have truly been saved.
God, I ask that you bless all my friends who are here
praying together now,
and I ask that you continue to lead life.
We love you!
In your precious names we pray.

Amen.

1

PRAYER TO LIFE L'CHAIM

Every time I sit to write my words land on the page as a song, a poem, a prayer to life -
L'Chaim!
But why?

What's the purpose for these words and for these rhymes?

Is this Gods sense of humor with me to not take it too seriously,

to keep it light, joyful and loving?

I would say so. Oh, it feels so good to write this poetry.

Like a breath of fresh air, so

I can get these thoughts out of me,
and into the world

living
somewhere
outside of my body.
        This feels important to share,
        as if my expression is that of others as well.
        My experience of these words feels familiar,
        like they aren't just mine
        but can be shared by anyone to relate to.
        You see, life *is* universal
        and we're all walking a path.
        Predestined, perfect, powerfully
unique and
intentionally inspiring.

2

ALIVE

I am
alive
Living
in light

God is
working miracles
in my life

Thanks be to God
for the blessings
I am so grateful
for what he brings

He's favored me
truly
and for that

I will sing

He will forever be mine
I am
Alive
Living
In light.

3

MADE RIGHT

Please
heal his heart
And also heal mine
Lord I pray
you reconcile
What was never
made right

Thank you for this day
For you
God
have made
the way.

And you have
shown me today
That my choice was not in vain

To grow
To know
To show myself to me
deeper than ever more

For there is no greater love than can be explored
I am at peace in this strength
I am at peace
in holy spirit
It has made

I can see the light
Towards the right
The way
With every new day
he hath made

The God who creates
the universe,
Wants to show me how it works.
The world that holds us tight
Can never create the light without
Christ.

4

SHIELD

It often feels like I'm unsure of how I feel
Like I've trained myself to not share or reveal
So that I can remain protected from judgement
Like a spiritual
shield.
Staying in situations that do not serve
the best
for all involved
is the reason
I feel drained
and so unsure for so long.
It's important that I be as honest as possible
about how I am offering
myself
and my energy –
and this will explain
a lot about how I feel and how to make the most

out of most.
I'm so tired of feeling lack luster
disappointed
By things that are great or good enough as
God only and always gives
– not takes –
but replaces
what we want
with what we need
to be most aware, alive, and awake
Help me God to be
more like you
and to
trust
what I
know, think, and feel to be
true.

5

CALLING

Why do I feel so unsure of my place in the world?

What am I supposed to do
with my life
for others
for me to serve.

I am feeling ready to be
in a state of prosperity

And to finally get my calling
from God with clarity

All I want to do
is make music
and offer our father mother praise

To be in my poetry and pray
And to cook
and express myself
culinarily

What is the value of my desires interests and passions

How can I hear
my true
purpose?

Is it to share my story
of loss
pain
and grief

To honor what I overcame.

Where do I begin
Again, and again, and again.

6

AGAIN

I had it all
But I let it go
Again, and again, and again

Why can't I hold it all though?
The pain of loss can't be for nothing
What does God want me to know?

What is here today
To show me my way
Will I trust in the Lord?

Nothing that is meant for me
Will leave if it is not meant to be
Spirit show me the purpose of it all

Got me

God's got me
I am worthy
valuable
empowered
Free.

Thank you for this opportunity.

7

LIVING

What a wonderful life
I am, you are, we're all
Living.

So much
I've experienced
So much
You've seen.

Sometimes I wonder
what it's growing
In me
For me
As me
To be

God, you're guiding this life,

so precious.

Thriving within a perfect plan
Breathing through all life's lessons
Seeing it clear now as beautiful blessings.

Nothing is a mistake since fear is fake
Love is all there really is.
Understanding this and knowing `
Is the holy ticket to paradise with Christ.

When we accept the miracle
To see and witness Heaven here and now
On earth and beyond
Surrounding us
everywhere and always
This is
spiritual business.

8

FEELING

Whoa I'm feeling
so much uncertainty
Over my relationship with family
With old friends
Of what used to be
While green and living.
My heart is hurt
How can I heal it now?
turns out
its only God that can
satiate me
I feel overwhelmed by my sadness
And my Greif stricken self
And yet I know
I'm here for a reason –
For holy spirit
Is helping me

Navigate
Make sense of
And understand
My dark
Season.
I want to let go of my past
But hold onto what it meant to get
To where I got. Yet
The disappointment
I know
In my heart of hearts
Was too loud to bear
Since it was me
I forgot.

9

BLESSINGS

Whoa blessings
On blessings
From every lesson
God thank you for being my example
Of flesh
And the divine human(e)
All of it living
Freely
Abundantly
Through and as Christ
Consciously
Awake
Let it go.
Be at peace.
Awake
In awe
Of the miracles

Surrendering
Receiving
Being the light
Living
Free
Thank you for making me.

10

ALIGNMENTS

Hello, from Harvard! I made it world.

[From
Antioch
Brentwood
Moraga
Buenos Aires
Chicago
New York City
Walnut Creek
San Francisco
Oakland
Los Angeles
Costa Mesa
Honolulu
Long Beach]

I am in awe of the alignments.

Words can't yet describe all that I'm feeling

But suffice to say this moment

Is sacred!

God is working through my life.

As I sit in orientation today it became very clear to me

That I have truly

Been

Given

A gift in my ability

To inspire

Impact in the modern world.

Something about my combination of being and seeing

the world through

My lived experiences

Has caused a confidence

In me that breathes

Truth

Warmth and

Holy conviction.

My story has become a miracle to others when I share.

My past was not for nothing.

What I am here to do

is help others be healthy.

11

PEACE AND PRESENCE

It's felt so up and down,
So unstable and unclear here.
I knew it wouldn't be each or perfect.
Yet I'm committed
to the process.
I'm feeling my way
through every day.
But what is it that I want to do with it now?
Where am I taking this?
What am I here to do?
When will it become clear?
What will it take for me to live at the level I know I'm
capable of?
Why do I hide myself and my beauty and my mastery?

I know so much and I have so much to say to help
people.
But sometimes I feel I can't help myself. Why not?
Is it my traumatic past and present,
that prevent me
from my own peace and presence?

I am so clearly special and kind and yet I feel I don't
believe in myself.
I feel unworthy of my greatness now
But I want to tap into the real me who's been begging to
come through.
The version of me that is big and bold and consistently
happy, free and unbothered by my trauma's past.
I will heal myself now because God wants me to thrive.

12

ONE LIGHT

Thank you, sis,
For the signs

Thank you, sis,
I can write

Thank you, sis,
I can sing

Thank you, sis,
I can rhyme

I can
do
anything

Thank you

God
For bringing her home
From earth
as it is
in heaven

I will fight to
share her light
her legacy
and her life.

As a symbol of Christ.
And of every living being
That comes from
One light.

13

ALIGNED IN OUR BIRTHRIGHT

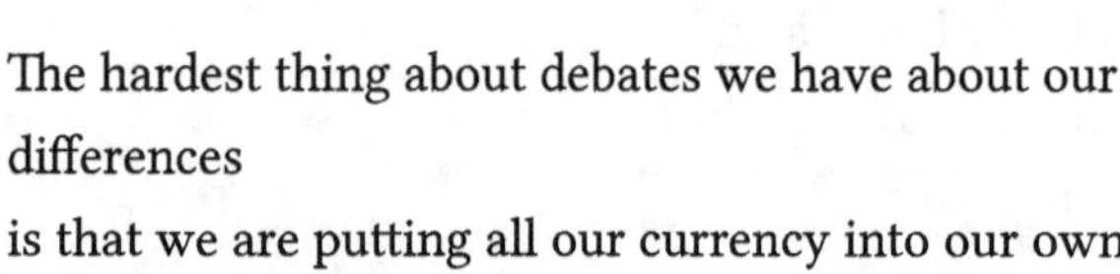

The hardest thing about debates we have about our differences
is that we are putting all our currency into our own
stupid superficiality that grips
our hearts and minds from being in connection
and aligned in our birthright.
And no matter your belief,
this consciousness is created from and as Christ.
None of our differences matter at the end of the day.
At the end of the day,
when we each put our bodies to rest every night,
then as G-d does at the end of our lives,
what we want is ourselves.
And what we long for is us reflected in each other,

in the parts and pieces, we know and the shadows
that are unknown to be seen by another.
It's a miracle that our world can move forward at all
anymore,
when you are you
and they are them,
but really,
we might ought to ask,
who is who.
And why do we want to believe this illusion as true.
Why were we given the ultimate model of being
both fully human and fully divine just to remain in
disbelief
of the possibility, power, and purpose of what this can
and does mean.
This, the oneness, is in us, too.
In and as and of each of us.
Us truly as One under the sun, the light - we are each a
hue.
Daughters and dudes and all sentient beings of the Great
I am.
One body.
Perhaps we are one consciousness manifest in many
forms so we can recognize each of us as ourselves.
Perhaps the thing that bugs you about the other is the
thing you reject in yourself.
Think about that for a second.

Why are you so upset about who they are or what they
did?
And in the power of your greatness and in your mind's
eye, isn't it true that you could not see that thing in them
that you dislike so much, if you didn't also somehow
recognize it in you.
But in each moment,
we have a choice, a breath, a single moment to
remember
this truth.

14

WILD RIDE

What a wild ride
indeed.
God help me see clearly.
What is next for my life?
My vocation is being determined
Partnerships and Purpose
In my everyday actions, relationships, and my Higher
education.
I need the spirit/ holy ghost to help me and strengthen
my mission and my focus for what is Driven.
What is it?
How come I'm stuck in the same interactions again and
again?
I am ready to be revealed by my work and my life's
calling to be in service.
Help me holy spirit, Jesus, and our Father to guide every
step of my way.

I need your support now more than ever before.
Without my lives prior, I would be more of a soft
Shell of myself
Learning and uncovering together.
Thank you for your help and guidance.
Keep speaking directly to me to point my target
at the right bullseye
For school, work, and relationships – show me the way.
And please make it clear because it must be easy.
You are incredible and I will always fight to share the
memory of Christ in and through my life.
From new expressions, I am being taught how to work
through and integrate the real me
Nowadays after I've weathered the storm.
Grateful for all I know and feel and
Trust today more than any other time before.
Please keep revealing my work to me and
How I'm meant in this world to be my best.
And my best is only ever available through my love and
devotion for Jesus. :)

15

DEAR GOD, DEAR ME

Dear God, Dear Me
Looking at the California sunset on the first of 2024
A new year indeed
I vow to move into this next new evolved chapter of my
life with my family friends and all who Know me.
I choose this year to work with my gut, my intuition, to
listen
To God inside talk to me
And lead me into what is next.
I have no idea
How to do this
on my own.
Lord shoe me how.
I need the steps to take,

the words to say,
to show me I am healthy and
liberated
Joyful and at Peace.
God show me, please.
It is so
Beautiful
to see and feel you in the sunset,
In the song,
in the sounds of my life and my love and
My devotion
To something greater than my past and pain,
and waiting for me to tap into
for my purpose.
Give me the information I need to make this
happen, easily, with compassion
and completely care-free
confident with You leading me. Jesus.
I need your mercy and grace to cleanse me from my
mistakes and to heal my wounds every day.
Thank you for speaking to me, through me, and continue
to use me.
I am nothing without your guidance and the power you
have placed in the plan you have for me. What is it, God?
Where? How? When? Reveal it ALL to me please.
I need the specifics shown to me in perfect awareness
that this is coming from you to me.

Thank you holy spirit, for helping me now surrender
fully, wholly, with and for you.
Forever I will praise your name!

16

ALL THREE

Holy Family,
How I love thee.
All three.
An ode to each of you as we begin this heal within our
wealth.
40 Days we have to rest repair and collect our whole
health.

Christ is coming back,
and we are being asked t
o come together
and connect.

To release
the racket,
the story,
the illusions

of fear
hurt
confusion of the fires of death.

To resurrect
us to ourselves,
as a holy family,
one body,
one bread
as the chosen living breathing.

Thank you for the strength in this prayer
for transformational and deep vital repair
We bow to your feet to surrender
our hearts to God our Father for the answer
Inside allow the Holy Spirit to awaken our inner
shadows we hide
To deliver them to the divine
for connection in the heart soul and mind
The spirit in son working in tandem.

17

FINAL DAYS | AIRES

Final Days
before I go back
and graduate.
Thank you, Jesus, for giving me the strengths to get
through this final push to fulfill my academic dream
even though I would not and did not know it would be
this awe inspiring!
So perfect God what you have continues to provide for
me – in ways that are better than I could have guessed
on my own, but with you,
Lord, You lift up my life and make it bright.
As shiny and sparkly as possible, turning my pain into a
diamond that is perfect and transformed in the fire to
reveal my brilliance and light.

Only you father could make this possible for us as your
children.
You provide all there is for us every single day, and in
every way – your divine
Might and purpose calling me and all of us into the plan
for our holy lives.
Thank you, God.
We feel you and know you and trust you fully.
I accept you as my savior and trust you fully as your love
is greater than anything else possible.
I'm grateful that you've taught me how to receive
Fully the gifts you have for my life and our world.
It is only what I've overcome with you that now I see
it's only possible through my surrender to
your guidance your direction your calling over me.
Every blessing working together to allow the best
possibility to reveal itself to me.
All things working together to bless me!
Together we are working side by side to reveal the best
The blessing in the storm,
To finally see the light.
Jesus you are amazing in every way every day.
I will never stop sharing your praise in my time alive.
Grateful and overjoyed with peace and passion for and
to be
An example of you Christ.

What would it take for this to improve?
Would it require a big change or another big move?
Please help me Lord understand
You,
and how you are working it through.

Last night I dreamt about being in a controlled fire.
Only those that were brave enough to join had the
desire.
But what is it about the heat that makes it feel so dyer?
Why can't we stand the heat?
Why do the flames make us feel like we must defeat?
Like fire is something to win from and flee,
Aires.

But how could this possibly be
when it is one of the four
elements of this world,
so important
and oh so
unique.

You see,
fire has the ability
to take over when not in balance

with air ether and water.
But did you know it's in
the power
of waves
of sound
for it to finally
and fully
extinguish.

This is new technology
and understanding
about firefighting,
that it requires more of dance with sound to be put out.
As for me, I feel the same sometimes,
waiting for the chance to dance in order to change.
I bet you can relate.

18

FREE FROM THE FIGHT

I'm free from the fight
for my life,
now aware
of the unending light
inside.

Noticing all the green
and all things
and living
beings.

Floral incense and
fresh air floating
weightlessly.

Birdies being
joyful and sounding
cute and flirty.
My grounding.

Feeling happy.

19

Use this Page | Changed

It's time to use this page
And fill this space.
Going back in time
In my writing
With the divine
Writing here
After
I'm nearing the end of this creative diary.
So much shared within me
Through
The
Heart
To
The

Mind and 3-D plain
On this page
By hand
With a pen.
Such a free feeling
Really.
So incredible to feel
The energy pulsing
Through my
Wrists
And my little tight
Fingertips.

There's so much that's changed
Yet somehow in many ways it still feels the same.
I feel like I am very often living in the old way over and
over again
But its tough to tell if it's important and if this was to be
avoided.
At this moment, a year after the war in the middle east
began, a year after the polarizing issue that is the anti-
Christ crisis.
That is the world we live in.

But together at the table can we see each other

As holy brethren
Breaking bread is.
The only thing that heals.
There is one truth which is love
Is Universal.

Together we can heal the world
One by one as we awaken
That holy peace is within
Beyond
Above
Is where we live.

20

NEW YEAR NEW MIRROR | OBSERVE

Already four days in and all I already want to quit
My thoughts keep spinning because my mind is full of shit
The only thing that will save me is the power of Jesus and the Holy Spirit

Make me whole
Keep us known
So that I don't have to revert back to the norm
Only you Lord are the power that is solely in control

What will it take for us to get through?

This world is a big blue ball of deep seeded fear
God protect our hearts and release our minds from the
lie that you aren't near
For the fruits of our life will indicate what is our work
and our ultimate mirror

What we reap we will sow
What we plant in life and with time, don't forget it will
grow
Rest in that which is the only power for more
Building the Kingdom is the only place we will ever
really soar

Thank you, Lord,
Thank you, God
Thank you
forever.

Tomorrow I go to the boat for the
Sea Trial.
We will
Turn it on
And come ready
To ask all the important questions
And to learn by how we

Observe...
We will listen
Within
And around
To know if this is it.
It feels like it is.
From the moment I stepped foot within...
And gazed aboard.
Lord will you be our captain.
Thank you, Christ.
You charter our path on
The right side of
Our father
And mother earth.
Let thy sun
Lead us through
To you
And to
the moon
as the divine feminine
our holy spirit
our intuition.

21

FOR THE BEST | BENEDICTION

Gratitude
for the Best
attitude:
I'm focusing on what I can control and that is all,
For that's possible.
I feel
Happier today than I am used to
Because I lean completely on Christ for his
Guidance
And his compassion
Mercy
And grace
What's it going to take
To see it through

To the end?
What's it going to be to remember
this isn't a race
But an important and practical survival place.
In your peace and in your worthiness
I finally feel and know my purpose.
Thanks for thank chance
To see how it changes lives and
Aids as a holy fortress.
It's amazing how much time passes but you kept it slow
and gentle for me
just as I prayed for and requested.
To move at your pace God, is the only speed for me
really.
I have tried to move it faster but I can't.
God is keeping me in and on track,
Adjusting my pace
And my power to meet his with
A bigger purpose,
To be for the betterment of all,
To be in
service.

Closing Prayer
Benediction

In the name of the Father Mother, Son and Sis, and loving Holy Spirit;

Thank you for allowing my words of this good word to
penetrate into the heart of this listening family
What an honor Lord to speak your righteous
and just truth.
For these poems to preach right through.
Only the one holy truth.
In Jesus we thank you

May life and light meet you through Christ.

Lord in your precious name give us the wisdom
from thy holy plate within.
Let us not catch fish, but catch men as brethren of one
holy world and body! Go vegan.

Amen.